SCAMS

SCAMS

A Resource Guide

SHELBY WAGNER

ISBN: 9798397659499

DEDICATION

This book is dedicated to all American veterans as a thank you for their service to our country.

KNOW YOUR ENEMY

"If you know the enemy and know yourself, you need not fear the result of a hundred battles. If you know yourself but not the enemy, for every victory gained you will also suffer a defeat. If you know neither the enemy nor yourself, you will succumb in every battle." [1]

— Sun Tzu, The Art of War

CONTENTS

INTRODUCTION

What is a scam?

> A **scam** is a term that describes
> any fraudulent business or scheme
> that takes money or other goods from
> an unsuspecting person... A person
> who does a scam is a scammer. [2]

There are more than a thousand different scams, and more are created every day. In 2022 – 2023 banks are reporting an increase in the number and financial losses their customers are losing. Unfortunately, the privacy of the internet makes catching scammers difficult.

I was inspired to write this book because I was scammed, and I decided to share my story so others can avoid losing their money to a criminal/or losing money in this way. Nothing would make me happier than for people to stop sending money to these criminals, for I believe, that is the only solution to ending this illegal business.

There are over a thousand different scams, and more are being created every day. This little book will help you recognize a scam when you see one. Consider keeping it nearby to remind you of this huge problem and share its contents with your family.

How big a problem is it? The Federal Trade Commission recently reported the following statistics.

- In 2017 approximately 1 in 5 Americans lost a portion of their hard-earned cash to a scam, and 2.7 million fraud reports were filed. [3]
- More than $5.8 billion was lost to scammers in 2021, a 70% increase over 2020. [4]
- Thousands of Americans are now struggling with strained budgets and/or broken hearts because of this illegal business and the emotional and psychological after-effects of being a scam victim.
- Financial loss to romance or confidence scams as reported by some agencies reached $1 billion in 2021, which made it the costliest of all scams reported. [5]

I have heard many people comment that they don't understand how anyone could be "so gullible" and proudly boast that "it would never happen to them!"

However, I know from experience that scammers are masters of manipulation. They learn their victim's weaknesses and use them to get what they want, which is money. Victims are brainwashed and almost hypnotized, and do not realize what is happening until it is too late.

I learned from experience that bank tellers are being trained to recognize certain symptoms that scammer victims exhibit.

Several men have told me they have sent money to a stranger on the internet, but they consider it a donation. However, when they told me their story, it was obviously the same story scammers use.

Since I was scammed, I have listened to several high-pressure salesmen who have reminded me of my scammer. I think scammers attended the same sales training.

If a high-pressure salesperson has ever talked you into buying something you didn't intend to buy, then you will understand a little about what a scammer's victim has gone through.

Have you ever purchased a "free vacation" and then spent hours of that vacation listening to a sales presentation? Multiply what you were feeling at that time by one hundred and you will experience some of what a scammed victim feels. Perhaps you could feel some sympathy for these victims.

Suggestion:

Keep this book handy so when you get a phone call or text message you don't recognize, you will be reminded to be careful.

Chapter 1 – Death Threat Scams

I am starting with this scam because I recently received one. Early one Friday morning as I was checking my messages, my eye was drawn to an interesting flash across the top of my cellphone screen. Investigating, I found the words, "Shelby Wagner, I am a really bad person. Someone you really don't want to know."

Unfortunately, I am a very curious person and my curiosity has gotten me in trouble many times. I must say, I was very curious this time. I clicked on it immediately, without even considering that I shouldn't.

> *"I don't know what you did to this person," the message continued, "but he or she has offered to pay me $1500 to eliminate you. I know all about you, where you live, your friends, etc. and you can believe that I will kill you! However, everything I read about you tells me you are a nice person and don't deserve to die. I have decided to spare you if you will pay me only $500. You must not show this to anyone or tell anyone about it. If you do, you will have a very painful death as will anyone who happens to be with you at the time. You must get the $500 to me asap. We will communicate through this app. Do not delete it…"*

How is that for a message, first thing in the morning? I must tell you it made me nervous. Yes, it was scary. As far as I know I have no enemies. I wrote back, “I don’t have $500.”

He responded, “It is $500 or your life.”

I reminded him that it was Friday, and the banks were going to be closed all weekend. He agreed to give me until Monday to get the money together, and he would contact me then.

What would you have done? I was pretty sure it was a scam. $1500 seemed low pay for killing someone, and why would this person accept $500 to spare me when he could have $1500 if he eliminated me?

I had a dentist appointment that morning and pondered my problem while in the dentist’s chair. By the time the dentist was finished with me, I had decided I would go to the local police.

The officer there assured me it was a scam and told me to block the number on my cellphone, which I did. All weekend I was watching over my shoulder, aware of my surroundings.

On Monday, I received an email from the scammer asking me who I had talked to and told me I should not have blocked him on my cellphone. I did not answer the email. A few minutes later, I received a phone number I did not recognize. It was from Canada. I did not answer the call, but I wrote down the number before I blocked it.

I admit I was spooked for a couple of weeks. My family was upset, and I was on alert to my surroundings. I even told my neighbor to keep an eye out for strange cars in the neighborhood, etc. Nothing else happened. I am still alive, thank God, but it was an unnerving experience.

My advice? Don't answer your phone unless you recognize the number.

Chapter 2 – Phone Scams

These calls are super annoying. Sometimes I get several in a day. The annoying part is that I am usually in the middle of something and tend to pick up the phone to hear a caller rattling off his/her name and company so quickly I cannot understand, and they do not stop until they ask, "Can you hear me, okay?"

That is when I hang up, because I know if I say "yes," I am giving them permission to continue. It would be better had I not answered the call.

Below are some common warning signs that you are talking to a phone scammer.

- A claim that you have been specially selected for something.
- Use of high-pressure sales tactics and "limited time" offers.
- The caller ignores your questions about the business or offer.
- A request for you to "confirm your personal information".
- A request for payment by means other than a credit card – such as cash, gift card, wire transfer or private courier.
- A request for your credit card number or other payment mechanism for "shipping and handling".

- Use of threats if you don't comply – even the threat of arrest.
- The call starts with a prerecorded message. – called a "robocall".
- A request for your log in information so the caller can fix a problem on your computer caused by a virus.
- The caller claims to be a friend or relative in need of money – and is urging for your quick compliance.

Here are some examples of Phone Scams.

<u>Tech Help Scams</u>

In these scams, the caller tells you that your computer has something wrong with it and they need remote access to repair the problem. You probably haven't even noticed your computer has a problem. It doesn't. Hang up the phone. End the call. This caller is attempting to access your computer so he/she can steal your personal information or install something malicious. Never allow someone who called you to do a remote access on your computer.

Don't ever allow anyone you don't know and trust to take control of your computer. End the call immediately and block the number if you can.

On the other hand, if your computer has a problem and you contact a technician that you know is reputable, then it is okay to allow them access.

Remember the saying, “If it ain’t broke, don’t fix it.”

Another thing to remember if someone calls you and says they are from Microsoft, or some other company you recognize, don’t believe them. Reputable companies like Microsoft never call their customers. Do not fall for this scam.

Credit Repair Scams

These callers offer to help you with your credit card debt, offering a low interest rate, or something similar. There is always a catch. Beware!

You do not know if the person calling you is telling you the truth or not. The only way to find out is to ask them the id number and name, then call the company yourself with a number you find online, call, and tell them you are calling to verify some information given to you by someone who called you.

There are legitimate programs that can help you with your credit card debt, but you must verify that the caller is who they say they are. Better still, hang up the phone.

Charity Scams

These callers ask for donations to help people who are ill or are in desperate need. The problem is those who need the money will never see it. If you want to donate money to an organization, make the donation directly to the organization. That way, you will know the money went where you intended.

One man gave a donation of $200,000 to a woman who called him on the phone asking for a donation to a charity she supposedly was representing. The woman and the money disappeared.

Extended Car Warranties –

These scammers are trying to sell overpriced or worthless car warranties. I still receive calls to buy an extended warranty for a car I sold eight years ago.

Grandparent (or good friend in trouble) Scams -

The caller will say he/she is calling from the police station where your grandson, Johnny, has been arrested for having drugs in his possession. Johnny needs you to send $2,000 right away so he can be released from jail. It is a lie. Johnny is at home in bed.

A variation on this type of scam is a call or email saying someone you know or related to a friend of yours is in Europe and needs $5,000 immediately. Call your friend or someone else who knows them well to check this out. Probably that person is at home and doesn't need the money at all.

Suggestions on dealing with phone scams.

1. Don't answer phone calls unless you recognize the number.

2. If you do answer, hang up the phone or end the call as soon as you don't recognize the company name.

3. If you answer, hang up when you hear the question, "Can you hear me okay?"

4. Use call blocking - Your phone carrier may provide a service to block known spam numbers or at least ID them for you when your phone rings. If you have a cellphone, you can block the number yourself. Ask someone you know to show you how to do this.

5, Don't rely on caller ID as proof of a scam. Phone scams have gotten better at making you think it is a legitimate number by "spoofing" an ID and displaying some type of official name. Some people even report seeing their own number in the caller ID.

6. Learn the red flags that tell you, “This is a scam.” Any time you hear the words “right away” or “immediately” you know that it refers to a scam. Hang up!

7. File a complaint through the FBI’s Internet Crime Complaint site. [https://www.Internet Crime Complaint Center (IC3)]. Your filing will be routed directly to the correct law enforcement agency.

Below is a list of phone scams that have been used in the past. Sometimes they are recycled, so be careful of them.

Fountain Blue Pools Text message – v6fvc info scam.

National Insurance Suspension

DMV Refund Scam (Dept of Motor Vehicles)

U.S. Marshals Scam Call USPS Text Message Scam

One-Ring Callers – the goal is to get you to call them back

Lottery Scams

Double-Dipping Scam

Health Care Debt Scams

Holland and Lieberman Lawsuit
Cadbury Hamper Scam

Wiggins Adjustments

HMRC Scam Call: Press 1 for your Tax Evasion Case

STD Check Text Message

Viber Scams

Phone Call from Mauritania Read More

Free iPhone 11

Old Friend Calling Scam

Calls from South Sudan

SIM Card Swap Scam

Fingerprint and Touch ID Scam

If You Receive a Call from Your Own Number, Do Not Answer it

Port Out Scam – tries to obtain your banking information

Calls from Numbers that look a lot like yours – spoofing calls

Free Nursing Home Stay

Forwarding Your Phone Access Scam

Free Cruise

Calls from Tonga Scam (676) 848

Bank of Ireland Text Message

Claim Back Bank Charges

Email Account Hack with Mobile Phone

Juice Jacking: Phone Charging

IRS Telephone Via VoIP Scam

First Page on Google Business Listing Calls

Civil Complaint Against You
Paramedic Call

WeChat Scams or Weixin

Caller ID Number Spoofing – looks like a bank, police officer or another trusted organization.

Line App Text Message Scam

Investigation Phone Call Scam

Your Bank Card is Not Working

Fake eTransfer Text Message

Kik Freebie Scams

M15 Security Scam

Counterfeit Money Call Scam

Fake Groceries for Seniors Scam

Fake Discount Phone Call

TV Promotion Scam

Inmate Release

Bluetooth Interception

Credit Union Account Unlocked

Fake Do Not Call Registry

Fraud Protection Agency Call Scam

Property Watch Offer

Bankers' Association Refund

TV Channels Upgrade

Call from Sheriff's Office

Copy Machine Call

Shares vs Carbon Credits

Malware Attacks on Android Phone

Utility Bills Paid by Federal Assistance

iPhone6 Tester Scam
Veterans Outreach Center Impersonators

Utilities Fake Rebates

Ringtone Download

Reimbursed Bank Fees

Somebody Hit your Car

Submit Corporate Minutes

Sticker for Traffic Tickets

Telephone Line Technician Scam

TTY Scams

Wrong Number Voicemail

Yellow Pages/411CanPages

Your Employee is in Jail

Jamaican Area Codes: 809, 87d6, 284

Jury Duty Absence
Living in Mexico Scam

International Calling Cards Fraud

Lottery Winning Call or Email

Lower Interest Rate

Microsoft Tech Support

Military Family Member

Pacquiao Show Text Message

Payday Loans

Pet Found Reward

Phone Interview Request

Pills Bought Illegal

iPhone Cases Recall: A Glittery Scam

Police/FBI Set UP

Red Light Tickets

BBB Fake Employees

Calamity Victim Waiting List

Card Inactive or Frozen

Cell Phone Radiation Protection Scams

Collect Call from Prison

Collection Call: Phone Bill Not Paid

Collection Call: Subscription

DEA Call

Customer Appreciation Call

Vax Box

Economic Stimulus

Civic Recognition Award Scam

Air Miles/WestJet/Expedia Fake Points

Scammer Phone Number Lookup: The Finder Trick

Chapter 3 – Advance Fee Scams

An advance-fee scam is one of the most common types of confidence tricks. The scammer typically promises the victim a significant share of a large sum of money in return for a small up-front payment. The fraudster claims the down payment will be used to obtain the large sum. If a victim makes the payment, the fraudster either invents a series of further fees for the victim to pay or simply disappears.

I have received several of these types of scams, supposedly from people I know. The money was supposedly coming from the US government in the form of a grant. That meant I did not have to pay it back.

I decided to test the system for $25, which I paid.

The FedEx truck had an accident on the way to my house. I was then asked to pay more money to transfer the package to another truck.

Save yourself some time and a headache. Just block the call.

Chapter 4 – Chat Scams

Watch out for unexpected text messages that you don't understand. They may be aimed at obtaining your personal information, like your password, account number, or Social Security number. Common chat scams include the following:

Fake Package Delivery

The text may offer a malicious link to confirm account details or ask for personal information. Do not click on the link printed in the message. Instead, retype the URL into a new browser address bar and click on it.

Free Prizes

These are the "too good to be true" announcements that you've won money, expensive watches, or handbags. You must give them your personal information to receive the prize. Do not do it.

Student Loan Assistance

Any kind of unsolicited debt repayment assistance should be viewed skeptically and confirmed independently from the sender.

Payment Processing Problems

Be wary of texts saying a payment didn't go through, especially if it asks for account information to approve the payment. Call your bank or the store to verify.

How to Deal with Chat Scams

Avoid chat fraud by verifying the message via a different source. For example: If a friend, family member, bank, or any other business asks you for personal information or money, validate the request by hanging up the first call and then calling the company from a number that you know is correct and ask about the person who called you.

Beware of unknown or strange numbers and ignore them.

Chances are, you already have the number of a friend or family member stored in your phone under their name. Verify the number you see on your cellphone's screen with the number in your "Contacts" list. Don't answer if you don't recognize the number.

Poor Grammar – Improper grammar in a text or chat message is usually a tip-off that it was written by a foreigner or it's a bot. Do not click on it. Block it.

Be safe, not sorry. If you do not recognize the sender of a message, ignore it. The safest response is no response at all. If the request is legitimate, the company or acquaintance will attempt to contact you in another way.

Chapter 5 – Web Scams

The anonymity of the internet makes it easy for scammers to trick you into giving away your valuable private information. It is important to be alert when using a computer or a phone. Do not allow your mind to be preoccupied and if an email or message looks strange to you, do not open it. Unless you initiated the conversation, do not fill out a form that asks for your private information.

Fake Commerce sites

Some websites sell stolen or fake products which are not worth the price paid requested and no delivery is intended. Phony retail websites are looking more real than ever. Do not click on an ad in an email or website. Instead, bookmark the URLs of trusted websites you use frequently and use them. Before you buy from a new website, check its online reviews and the company's track record at BBB.org. (Better Business Bureau's online directory.)

Auction Fraud

Some scammers launch websites pretending to sell a certain product that may not even exist or they have stolen from the real owner. Examples of this type of fraud are concert tickets and pirated software.[6]

Credit card fraud

Beware of websites that request your credit card number upfront. Legitimate websites require a username and password to access accounts, not your credit card number.

Malware

Software designed to damage your computer or disable it is called malicious malware. Malware is also a general term that refers to viruses, spyware, worms, trojans, and more.

Covid-19 Vaccination Card Scams

Many people have posted selfies on social media showing off their vaccination cards, and scammers have pounced on it, stealing information from the cards like full names, birthdays, and information locations where the shot was given. With this information, scammers have valuable data for breaking into your bank accounts, getting new credit cards in your name, and much more. Don't do this. Instead, use a "Got my Vaccine" picture frame on social media for your photo.

How to Avoid Web Scams

Keep your computer software updated.

Operating systems, web browsers, and apps are constantly being updated to adjust to the scammers' new tricks. You must update the apps and programs on your own computer. Take advantage of this service and update your apps often.

Buy only from trusted sources.

Do some research. If something feels strange or you are not sure of the website, do not use it. McAfee Web Advisor is a great resource for help in identifying some unsafe sites when you attempt to visit them.

Use only trusted sites. Look carefully at the URLs – a scam website will look like the real one, but there will be something that is different. Beware!

Talk to your kids, family, and friends.

Make sure everyone in your family is educated about the dangers of fraud on the internet. Teach them the red flags from this book and teach them **not** to answer the phone if they do not recognize the number.

Chapter 6 – Online Scams

The following scams are frequently found online but may also be encountered in chat rooms, text messages, emails, and on the phone. Common online scams include the following.

Prize Scams

You'll be notified that you just "won" a nice prize like money, jewelry, or a vacation, but you must pay something upfront. If you are asked to pay money to "win" something, you didn't win it; you bought it.

Crowdfunding Scams

Crowdfunding is the practice of funding a project or venture with money from many people, typically via the internet.[7]

"**Crowdsourcing** is the act of collecting services, ideas, or content through the contributions of a large group of people." This happens when many people are enlisted to give information or input into a project. People may be paid or unpaid. This occurs typically via the internet. [8]

Creators of the crowdsourced request promise a return for your small investment in their project but usually end up pocketing the money instead.

Payment through cryptocurrency

One sure sign of an online swindle is one requiring payment in cryptocurrency. Wire transfer, gift card, or cryptocurrency ensures that if you pay, there's almost no way for you to get that money back.

Online Survey Scams

These scams are survey sites that offer money or gift vouchers to victims for their opinions. Victims never receive any money, and the scammers have the information they sought from the victim.

Dark Pattern Scams

These scams are also known as a "deceptive design pattern". It is "a user interface that has been carefully crafted to trick users into doing things, such as buying overpriced insurance with their purchase or signing up for recurring bills."[9]

Avoiding Online Scams

If a prize you won is too good to be true, it probably is. Do your research about the contest with a browser search. Many times, you will find stories of others that have already been taken.

Never send money or gift cards to a person you have not met in person.

Research any crowdfunding campaigns to see feedback from others and if they have not delivered on their promises.

Always look for the security lock and/or the “s” in the URL if you are asked for personal information.

Chapter 7 – Phishing Scams

Many of us have seen or been the target of a phishing attack. These scams use websites similar to those used by reputable companies to trick you into giving them your personal and private information.

Phishing is often deployed through emails, website pop-ups, and even mobile apps. Common phishing scams include the following.

The Mobile Phish

Scammers distribute fake mobile apps that gather your personal information in the background or send text messages containing dangerous links.

File Sharing & DocuSign

Phony requests to access files in Dropbox and DocuSign accounts are on the rise, tricking workers into clicking on dangerous links. Do not click on the link offered. Instead, type it in the address bar and search for the site there.

Surveys

You get a request to take a survey for a social issue you may care about. When you click that link, you could get infected with malware.

The CEO/Executive

This scam appears as an email from a leader in your organization, asking for sensitive information like company accounts, employee salaries, Social Security numbers, and client information.

The Romance Scam

This one can happen completely online, over the phone, or in-person once contact is established. The romance scam almost always starts with someone supposedly looking for love by posting a profile and a stolen photo on a dating website, Facebook, or other social media. What starts as the promise of love or partnership often leads to requests for money or expensive gifts. The lure here is acceptance.

The Urgent Email Attachment

Phishing emails try to trick you into downloading a dangerous attachment that gives someone access to your computer. Such emails ask you to download attachments confirming a package delivery, trip itinerary, or prize.

Government Scams

Scammers pretend to represent the IRS or Social Security Administration. Anyone who calls and tells you they are a government department or agency is a scam. Just hang up. These organizations do not make phone calls asking for information, nor do they try to scare you by telling you that the police are on the way to arrest you for anything. It is simply not true.

HANG UP! END THE CALL IMMEDIATELY!

How to Avoid Phishing Scams:

Ask yourself:

"Do I know this person?"

Check to see if you recognize the sender's name and email address.

"Is this asking for too much information?"

Be wary of anyone who asks for more information than they need, even if you are talking to a company or bank, you do business with.

Is that a legitimate link?

If the text or chat does not use proper grammar, then it is a bot or a scammer operating from a foreign locale.

Am I on the web page I think I'm on?

Before logging in to an online account, make sure the web address is correct. Phishers often forge legitimate websites, like online storage accounts, hoping to trick you into entering your login details.

Is it too good to be true?

Avoid “free” offers or deals that sound too good to be true.

Is my security software active?

Always use online protection to secure your devices and personal information from malware and other threats associated with phishing scams.

Chapter 8 – Email Scams

The most common email scams involve phishing. Phishing schemes take on the appearance of a legitimate email. They may even appear to be from a company you're familiar with to exploit your trust and gain personal or financial information. Common email frauds include the following.

Foreign Lottery Scam

Notifications that you won a big prize, often in a foreign country, but you must pay a small amount upfront to gain the larger reward.

Survey Scam

You get a request to take a survey for a social issue you may care about. When you click the link, you get infected with malware.

Banking scam

You receive an email saying there is something wrong with your bank or PayPal account that needs your attention. You're then directed to a fake site where you attempt to log in so they can steal your username and password for the actual site.

Business Scams

Business Scams use email fraud to attack commercial, government, and non-profit organizations to achieve a specific negative outcome.

Examples include invoice scams and spear phishing spoof attacks designed to gather data for other criminal activities. Consumer privacy breaches often occur as a result.

The goal is to trick an official into approving payments that transfer money into the fraudster's bank account.

Chapter 9 – Other Scams

You receive e-mail claiming that a company has found something wrong with you or your company and is threatening legal action unless you pay. This is also called **ransomware**.

Chain Mail Scams

Usually harmless, but this scam spreads through e-mail and tells people to forward e-mails to all their friends to get money back from someone like Bill Gates.

419 [or Nigerian scam]

This scam gives the impression that a large amount of money can be had, but your bank information is required to deposit the money into your bank account. The bank information is used against you, or the deposits are kept with no reward.

Pump and Dump Scam

In a pump and dump scheme, fraudsters typically spread false or misleading information to create a buying frenzy that will "pump" up the price of a stock, and then the fraudsters "dump" shares of the stock by selling their own shares at the inflated price. Once the fraudsters dump their shares and stop hyping the stock, the stock price typically falls, and investors lose their money. [10]

Rug-Pull Scam

One common scam in the crypto space is called a "rug pull". In this scam, a developer or creator will promote a project, such as a new coin or NFT release, and then disappear with investor money. The perpetrators of rug pulls are difficult to track down after the fact, as the decentralized and pseudonymous nature of blockchain allows those involved to conceal their identities. [11]

Exit Scams

An **exit scam** is a confidence trick where an established business stops shipping orders but continues to receive payments for new orders. Customers who trust the business do not realize their orders are not being fulfilled until the business has already disappeared.[12]

A cryptocurrency exit scam is when the developers of a cryptocurrency pull their funds and abandon the project to profit from investors. An exit scam can occur before, during, or after a cryptocurrency is launched.

How to Avoid Email Scams

If you don't do business with a particular company or haven't requested information from a particular company, don't click on any links or take any surveys.

Look at the sender's email address. Does it match the content of the email? If not, stay away.

Avoid communications without personalization. If the email or letter begins with, "Dear valued customer," skip it.

Does the link in the email look odd? Most of the time, you can move your mouse over the link to see the link address. If it seems wrong, stay away.

Chapter 10 – Senior Citizen Scams

Senior Citizens are being targeted by many scammers for several fraudulent schemes. All seniors must become aware that they are at risk. The FBI has identified the following scams which specifically target the elderly.

Grandparent Scams

Criminals are posing as a relative—usually a child or grandchild—claiming to be in immediate financial need. The caller may also pose as police officers, detectives, etc.

Romance Scams [see Chapter 12 for more information about these Scams]

Criminals set up fake profiles and stolen photos to attract romantic partners on social media or dating websites with lots of attention, encouraging words, and visions of "happy ever after" to win the elderly victim's trust so they can steal their money.

Tech Support Scams

Criminals pose as technology support representatives and offer to fix non-existent computer issues. This may include posing as a cybersecurity company they're familiar with. The scammers gain remote access to victims' devices and sensitive information or bill them for services never needed or rendered.

Government Impersonation Scams

Criminals pose as government employees and threaten to arrest or prosecute victims unless they agree to provide funds or other payments.

Chapter 11 – Crypto Currency Scams

Cryptocurrency has become a common method for scammers to receive money from their victims. More than 46,000 people have reported sending crypto to a scammer since January 2021, according to the Federal Trade Commission.

In 2021, $680M in losses were reported, which is sixty times the loss reported in 2018. Most of these losses were investment frauds that involved cryptocurrencies. Scammers contacted victims on social media, started a conversation to establish trust, and brought up the subject of bitcoin or other crypto. They promised easy money to be made, which always attracts people.

Other reasons cryptocurrency scams are successful are as follows:

- There is no centralized authority to flag suspicious activity.
- Crypto transfers cannot be reversed as the money is automatically transferred into the scammer's wallet.
- Most people do not know how cryptocurrency investing works and are easily duped.
- Social media and crypto appear to be a good combination for fraud.

Crypto victims do not realize they are tracking their progress on fake investment company websites and apps. Whenever they attempt to withdraw their money, they discover they cannot because they must meet one or all of the following conditions.

- They must recruit others who make a deposit into their own fake accounts.
- Fake checks have been sent to their bank accounts which ruin their reputations and cause the bank to close their bank account,
- Once they comply with one condition, they will receive another.

They will never get their money back. It is a vicious circle designed to steal all their money.

If you are involved in this type of scam, stop communicating with them immediately and block them. If you do not, you will lose even more money.

Someone may contact you saying they can help you get your money back. This is a lie. They will just suck more money out of you!

Chapter 12 – Romance Scams

What is a Romance Scam? Wikipedia.org has the following definition.

> A romance scam is a confidence trick involving feigning romantic intentions towards a victim, gaining their affection, and then using that goodwill to commit fraud. Fraudulent acts may involve access to the victim's money, bank accounts, credit cards, passports, e-mail accounts, or national identification numbers; or forcing the victims to commit financial fraud on their behalf. In many instances, a mail-order bride scam will also bait the victim into committing felonies to establish citizenship for the perpetrator.[13]

Other names for this type of scam are dating scam, imposter scam, confidence scam, and Catfish.

According to an article in Forbes by Zachary Smith (2022/2/10), an FBI report stated, "About 24,000 Americans lost a reported $1 billion to romance scammers during 2021." The Federal Trade Commission reported 2021 as the most lucrative year for romance scammers on record.[14]

Journalist Smith also stated cryptocurrency is replacing the traditional ways of making payments to scammers, which were gift cards, wires, and money grams.

The request for money is the main red flag that tells you the person you are chatting with is a scammer. Today, cryptocurrency has become the payment of choice and that request is a major red flag of a scam. End all conversations immediately and report him/her to the administrators of the website.

Perhaps you are one who proudly proclaims you would never fall for this scam. Be careful. Never say never. Scammers are masters of manipulation, and they know how to get their victims to do whatever they ask. They know exactly what to say and do, and they do not give up until they win. They are very persistent.

Block them, or you will wish you had.

Scammers are criminals. They lie and steal photos of attractive people, create fake dazzling profiles, and post them on social media to lure unsuspecting singles longing for love and romance. Once a conversation is begun, the victim is showered with compliments, encouraging words, and visions of a fantastic and blissful future relationship. The objective of all this is to win the victim's trust so the criminal can get their victim to give them their money.

Be careful. Just because you have been chatting or texting with someone on the internet for a long time, you really do not know that person, even though it may feel like he/she has become a good friend. Unless you have met them in person many times, you do not know if the person on the other side of your computer is telling the truth or not. Sometimes, you may not even really know a person that you have met in real life. It takes doing things together to know someone.

Victims of scammers admit that they lose much more than their money. They lose the person they thought loved them and the dream which they invented. What else do they lose? They lose their dignity and self-respect and the respect of their families and friends.

Many people feel ashamed of their mistake and usually do not tell others that they have been scammed. They feel embarrassed and humiliated, and sometimes they even feel as if they are the criminal. Being a victim of a scammer ruins family relationships and friendships. Some victims have even been killed by their scammers.

Despite warnings about scammers in the media, the problem has grown so huge that it is an epidemic. This is a huge social issue people need to know about and talk about. The only way it can be stopped is for people to STOP giving them their money.

There is nothing wrong with wanting to find love. The desire to love and be loved is a basic human need. Love helps us to feel good and it helps us to feel happy.

Internet dating websites are a wonderful way to meet new people. But one must be careful. Do not tell strangers information about yourself that should be kept private. Your financial situation is no one else's business. Do not give someone you haven't met in person your log-in information to financial institutions. If you have already done so, change your passwords immediately. Do not send money to people you meet only on the internet.

A few people have told me they have never been scammed, then go further and brag that they gave money to someone on the internet. They think of it as a donation to someone in need. However, truth be told, they were scammed! Do not give money to someone who asks you for money unless you know them really well and have met them in-person. People lie. If someone asks for a loan, most likely you will not get your money back. Just say no and stick to it.

Several months ago, I met an acquaintance in line, and we began chatting. He asked about my first book, Learning to Dance in the Rain – Surviving Grief, Internet Dating and Romance Scams, and then he confided he was scammed by a woman he met at the singles dances. She asked him to loan her $2,000 for a new refrigerator. He said he felt sorry for her and loaned her the money. He was never repaid, and he later learned she had spent the money on drugs. He felt used, and he felt awful! He was defrauded. Scams happen even in real life! It happens all the time.

Chapter 13 – Red Flags

Wondering if you are chatting with a scammer? Here is a list of red flags which I have compiled from experience that 99% of the time have occurred in my e-mails and text messages from guys who, a few days or weeks later, asked me for something, such as a gift card, sim card, or to wire them some money. They proved to be scammers.

The first three red flags below are immediate proof of a scammer. Stop chatting with them and block them immediately and report them to the website on which you met them.

1. Use of the words, **urgent**, or **send immediately,** with the request for money.

2. A request to move the conversation to another app, like WhatsApp, Google Chat, etc.

3. A request to send money, gift cards, or cryptocurrencies.

The following list tells you to go slow or be careful. Once you see more than two of the following red flags, stop talking to them and move on!

4. A request for your personal information too quickly.

5. If the sender claims to have his/her own business, to be an engineer, to work in construction, works offshore

on an oil rig, or is in the military or on a peacekeeping mission.

6. If anyone claims to live in the USA but is working in a foreign country.

7. If anyone lives extremely far from you.

8. If the sender is twenty to fifty years younger than you.

9. If anyone falls in love with you right away.

10. If a 75-year-old claims to have a 7-year-old son or daughter.

11. If the person's photo looks younger or older than the person claims to be.

12. If the photo looks like it may have been copied?

13. Are there any inconsistencies in their profiles?

14. Does the area code match where the person says he or she lives?

15. Does a background search support what they have told you?

16. Does their Facebook page or other Social Media support what they have told you?

17. Does their Facebook page show only a few friends and photos?

18. Have you been asked to stop communicating with others right away?

19. Does their name appear in a Google search?

20. Check out other social media sites. Does the information match what you have been told?

21. Does he/she always cancel a meeting date?

22. Does he/she fall in love with you before you meet in person?

23. Does the sender use a lot of poems, cute emojis, images, and links to love songs?

24. Do you recognize similar wording from more than one sender?'

25. If you have had a phone conversation, does the other person have a strange accent?

26. Are your calls answered personally or by an answering service?

27. Does their voice sound like they are talking "in a box"?

28. Does the voice sound disguised in any way?

29. Is there any background noise? Pay attention to it.

30. Are there people talking in the background?

31. Have you heard this voice before?

32. Are you asked, "How long have you been on the dating site, and what is your experience?" (May not be a red flag, but if it comes with other red flags, then it is.)

33. Are you asked, "Do you live alone?

34. Does anyone asks, "What are you doing now?" or "Where you are going now?"

35. If anyone asks, "Have you eaten breakfast [or lunch or dinner]?"

36. Has the contact person called you by the wrong name or misspelled your name?

37.Evidence use of poor spelling and/or bad grammar.

38. Are your questions being answered?

39. Does the sender tell you he/she makes a six-figure income or more?

40. Has anyone told you he/she owns several large and/or expensive homes or cars?

How to Deal with These Scams

1. Stop talking to anyone who exhibits more than three of the red flags above and block them. If they ask for

money or something you must buy and send to them, report them.

2. Do not click on links in emails or text messages, they may contain malware that will damage your computer.

3. Do not repeat passwords across accounts. If you do get tricked into giving away your password, fraudsters will use them to try to log into your other accounts.

4. When in doubt consult someone you trust. Scammers count on you being too emotional to think clearly. Always reach out to someone you trust – a relative or attorney – for a second opinion.

5. Stop chatting immediately if you see 3 or more red flags from the same person.

6. Block them and report them to the dating website and to the authorities.

7. If you are the victim of a romance scam, file a complaint with the FBI's Internet Crime Complaint Center immediately.

8. A request for a loan or iTunes card or cash is evidence of illegal activity. You must refuse those requests and block them immediately. Report them. You can report them at www.fbi.gov.

9. Report to your local police if you are being victimized in any way.

10. Do **not** send money to anyone you meet only online.

11. Do **not** give anyone your social security number, credit card numbers, or banking information.

12. Stay safe by withholding your last name, address, and/or phone number from people you do not know well.

13. Keep the names of your family members
private also. You do not know how strangers will use this kind of information.

Chapter 14 – Victims' Stories

In this chapter, I share some stories of victims I have talked with or read about on the internet.

Number 1—In July 2019, Dr. Phil's television show featured a woman whose two daughters sought Dr. Phil's help to convince their mother she was being scammed. The woman proved to be so entirely vested in her "romance" that she was convinced she was married to the actor Tyler Perry, even though she had never met the man. Here is how Dr. Phil advertised the show.

(https://www.drphil.com/shows/my-mom-is-delusional-she-thinks-shes-married-to-tyler-perry-and-has-sent-her-catfish-100000/)

Although Dr. Phil presented Karla with evidence that she was the victim of a scam, she was so sure of her romance that she refused to believe him. The only concession she made was that she would not send any more money to this man.[16]

~~~~~~~~

Number 2—My friend Judy confided to me that she was also scammed, not once but twice. She said she felt "stupid." I immediately replied, "You were not stupid. You were just vulnerable!"

Judy agreed that she was indeed vulnerable, and someone had taken advantage of her in that state. She continued with her story - when she realized she had been scammed, she
~~~~~~~~

contacted the FBI and was told she was one of several thousands of victims of romance scammers. She was also told she would probably not get her money back. The ensuing FBI investigation resulted in the arrest of the person who scammed her. He was a retired priest with Alzheimer's who was living in a nursing home in Germany. He claimed he had sent the money to his scammer, but that person was never found.

Judy admitted she felt stupid because this was the second time she had been scammed. The first time was by someone she knew, and she thought she should have learned from that mistake.

***

I told her that many victims say, "It is not just the loss of the money. Even more painful is the loss of self-respect and the knowledge that one has been taken advantage of in this way. A broken heart and the loss of a dream of fulfilled love is be devastating."

Being scammed is a humiliating event that one never forgets and one that is always "the elephant in the room" once family members discover that it happened.

~~~~~~~~

Number 3—Another person I met told me of her daughter's experience. She had dated a man she had met online for four years before she married him. Not long after their wedding, she noticed her savings account was dwindling, and she had not
~~~~~~~~

been making any withdrawals. Looking into the matter, she found her husband had been withdrawing money from her account without her knowledge. When he left for a business trip, she decided to see what she could learn about his activities on his computer. She was horrified when she learned he was still on several dating websites posing as a single man looking for not just any woman but a young teenager. She also found nude photos of young children in his desk drawer. She called the police and started divorce proceedings.

~~~~~~~~

Number 4—Women are not the only ones used by scammers. Cal shared his story with me. He had started a conversation with someone in a chat room. He began to suspect he was chatting with a minor and decided to try to find out for sure by setting up a meeting at a local park, He planned to drive by, and if he saw she was too young, he would drive by. When he arrived at the meeting place, he saw a police car, and he was arrested. What he learned over the next few years was that the officer broke the law by setting a trap for him. Had he known this earlier, he would not be considered a felon today.

~~~~~~~~

Number 5-- There was an article on the internet about a man who donated $200,000 to what he thought was a charity. However, the woman who convinced him to donate the money disappeared, and so did the money.

~~~~~~~~

Anyone who has not experienced being victimized in this manner will never fully understand how people can be so gullible. Neither do they realize they are causing those who did fall for the scam to feel as if they are the criminal. It is not a pleasant feeling.

A group called Advocating Against Romance Scammers (AARS) was created to help bring awareness about romance scams and how they have impacted the world today. Its website is: https://advocatingforu.com/.[17]
~~~~~~~~

Chapter 15 – The Battle Our Veterans Didn't See Coming

This information for this chapter comes from a brochure I found at the US Post Office. The brochure is a joint venture of AARP and the US Post Office to inform veterans they are at risk just like the public because of criminals preying on the vulnerable.

The brochure is called OPERATION PROTECT VETERANS and is published by the Fraud Watch Network. [18]

Our veterans' time on the battlefield is over. They spent many years protecting us. Now it's our turn to help protect them.

Our veterans are warriors trained to handle anything a battlefield can throw at them. But there's one foe many veterans struggle to defeat, and that is domestic fraud.

78% of our retired military men and women have been targeted by scams specifically crafted to exploit their military service history. Sadly, veterans are twice as likely to fall for fraudulent schemes than non-military personnel.

In 2017, AARP research found that 16% of veterans lost money to scammers, compared to only 8% of the non-military public.

Why is that?

For starters:

- Veterans implicitly trust fellow members of the military. This makes them vulnerable to imposters.

- Veterans also have a PTSD rate more than double the general public's, which makes it more difficult for them to recognize and combat the emotional manipulation used by scam artists.

Our veterans deserve a lot of things.
Praise. Honor. Security. Respect.

They do not deserve attempts to take advantage of their service. Yet every day, scammers attempt to defraud them of their hard-earned benefits, steal their identity, or take their savings.

Together, we can fight back and repay our veterans for the service they've given and the sacrifices they've made.

Now, AARP and the U.S. Postal Inspection Service are joining forces for **Operation Protect Veterans.**

We're fighting back against fraudulent scam artists – and we need everyone's help. Good intel is a crucial component of this battle. If you've seen a scammer targeting veterans in the past twelve months, please report it by calling 877-908-3360.

Chapter 16 – Know Your Enemy

Ways scammers target veterans:

VA Loan Scams

Offers to refinance VA loans at extremely low rates.

Update Your File Scam

An imposter, claiming to be from a government agency, attempts to get a veteran's personal information to "update their file" so they can maintain their benefits.

Secret Veteran Benefits Scam

Scammers tell veterans they qualify for "secret" government programs or benefits that offer thousands of dollars – but first, they must pay a fee or give their private information.

Aid and Attendance Scam

Scammers tell veterans (or their family members) to move their assets into a living trust so they can qualify for financial assisted-living benefits. This is not true.

Veterans also encounter the same scams aimed at the public, many of them have been described in this book.

Chapter 17 – In Summary – How to Protect Yourself

1 **Recognize urgency as a red flag**

Pause before you do anything. Phrases like "right now" or "there's no time" can be a clue that something is not right. Think before you act!

2. **Keep your security up to date.**

Hackers and scammers are constantly looking for ways to sneak past your security protocols and into your computer. That is why it is important to make sure your computer's security programs are updated yearly.

3. **Be sure to use a different password for each of your accounts.**

Scammers are not trying to guess your passwords until they get them right. Rather, they hack the security systems of big companies and once they've successfully discovered yours, they will attempt to use the password they get into all of other accounts. Try using a password manager site like LastPass, to safely encrypt your data.

4. **Do not use public WiFi networks to access your private banking information.**

Public Wi-Fi networks allow easy access to your information.

5. **Double-check email addresses**.

Scammers contact victims via email in which they pretend to be from a business or social media website you use and ask for you "to provide or confirm your personal details." This is called Phishing, and it is almost impossible to tell fake ones from authentic ones. Be sure to double-check every little detail in the email address of the sender. Since hackers can't create email accounts with the organizations they are pretending to represent, their email addresses are usually one or two letters different. For example, the email address service@targt.com, looks a lot like the real one service@target.com.

6. **Check for typos.**

Grammatical errors are typical red flags in an email because many of them are foreigners who often mix up English pronouns and verbs.

7. **Use longer passwords which are more difficult to crack**.

For example, instead of using the words baby blue, which is easily found in a dictionary, use something longer, such as babybluebuggieismyfavoritethingintheworld.

Even better is a combination of letters, numbers, and characters, which make absolutely no sense.

8. **Do not participate in online quizzes?**

Scammers use the information they get from your answers to hack security questions to your most sensitive accounts.

9. **Do you post sensitive information on your Facebook pages?**

All day, every day, hackers are scouring Facebook, Twitter, Instagram, and other social media sites to steal information that might be part of your password.

10. **Be careful, scammers are good at getting you to reveal sensitive information by claiming to be calling you from your bank or insurance company.**

Do not give a caller your passwords or credit card number on the phone. The same is true for so-called "free trips" for which you must pay a fee. If you get a call out of the blue about a deal that sounds too good to be true, that's because it is.

When in doubt, always call your credit card provider or bank directly to verify that they're the ones calling you before revealing any information about yourself—or better yet, just don't pick up from unfamiliar numbers at all. Instead, wait until they've left a message, Google the number they're calling from, and call back if need be.

11. Do you use SMS for two-factor authentication?

This is not recommended because SMS—the technology used for text messages—is relatively easy to hack. Instead, use an authenticator app, like Google Authenticator or Authy.

12. Do you ever shop on new websites without verifying their legitimacy?

According to the security site, www.asecureLife, your personal or financial information could be stolen, or your device could become infected with a virus or malware. Always confirm that the website begins with https:// before making a purchase. Only secure sites have this before their URL. Also, you can look up the name of the site on Whois.com to make sure that it's registered to a legitimate business.

13. Do not save your information on computers that are shared with strangers.

You never know who has access to that computer after you've moved on. Plus, you have no idea how secure the Wi-Fi network at your workplace is; for all you know, it could require little to no effort to hack it!

14. Do you accept Facebook friend requests from strangers?

According to the ACCC, scammers will sometimes set up fake profiles on social media sites to get to their victims. So, how does this work? A con artist can use a social media site to their advantage by luring someone into a fake relationship and then convincing that person to send them money. Other criminals will simply collect information available on your profile and through messaging with you until they have enough to either hack your accounts or assume your identity.

15. Do you empty your mailbox every day?

Opening someone else's mail might be a crime, but that is not stopping scammers from doing it anyway. Mail from your bank, credit card company, or the IRS could have everything from account numbers to your social security number on it, making it easy for scammers to steal your identity. And the longer you leave your mail out, the more vulnerable it is, so make sure to empty your box every single day.

16. That pop-up message claiming that you just won a free cruise to the Bahamas probably isn't real.

Rather, it's almost certainly a ploy by a scammer to get money or other information out of you. According to the Federal Trade Commission, you can usually tell whether a sweepstakes is a scam when you have to pay to enter or have to deposit the check you've won and then wire some of that money back.

17. Scammers often obtain information about you "through… discarded personal documents such as utility bills, insurance renewals, or health care records," warns the ACCC.

When you do need to throw out sensitive documents, your best bet is to put them through a shredder first. If you don't have a shredder, make sure to rip and destroy all of your papers until the information on them is no longer legible, or get a text-obscuring rolling stamp to cover up any sensitive information.

18. Never send a picture of your credit card to anyone - hackers may intercept it.

If you absolutely must give someone your account information, then do so over the phone; otherwise, meet up in person and you can avoid the possibility of a scammer accessing your information.

19. Consult someone you trust.

Scammers count on you being too emotional to think clearly. Always reach out to someone you trust—a relative or attorney—to get a second opinion. [19]

THE END

NOTES

1.Wikipedia, Sun Tzu, *The Art of War.*

2.Computerhope.com, *scam.*

3.cnbc.com, *Consumers lost 5.8 billion.*

4.cnbc.com, *Consumers*

5.Forbes, *Americans Lost $1 Billion.*

6.seon.io, *auction-fraud.*

7.Wikipedia, *crowdfunding.*

8.Wikipedia, *crowdsourcing.*

9.Wikipedia, *dark pattern.*

10.Investor.com, *pump and dump.*

11.Coindesk.com, *rug pulls.*

12.Wikipedia, *exit scam.*

13 Wikipedia, *romance scam.*

14.Wikipedia, *Smith.*

15.Wikipedia, *Smith.*

16.McGraw, *Dr. Phil shows Mom she is delusional.*

17. https://advocatingforu.com/

18.AARP.org, *fraudwatchnetwork.*

19.Yahoo.com, *17 ways making.*

BIBLIOGRAPHY

AARP Brochure, “Operation Protect Veterans,” accessed October 12, 2022. http://AARP.org/fraudwatchnetwork and United States Postal Inspection Service.2022.

Advocating Against Romance Scammers, accessed March 21, 2023, https://advocatingforu.com/.

Coindesk.com, “What is a Rug Pull and How to Protect Yourself from Getting Rugged,” accessed December 27, 2022, https://www.coindesk.com/learn/what-is-a-rug-pull-how-to-protect-yourself-from-getting-rugged/. 2022.

Computer Hope, s.v. “advance fee,” accessed December 18, 2022, https://www.computerhope.com/jargon/s/scam.htm. ??advance-fee??

CNBC.COM. “Consumers Lost 5.8 Billion to Fraud last year,” Accessed February 10, 2022, https://www.cnbc.com/2022/02/22/consumers-lost-5point8-billion-to-fraud-last-year-up-70percent-over-2020.html, 2022.

Computerhope._s,v, “scam,” accessed September 30, 2022, https://computerhope.com/jargon/s/scam.htm. 2022.

Forbes.com, Smith Zachary, “Americans Lost $1 Billion to Romance Scammers Last Year,” accessed February 10, 2022, https://www.forbes.com/sites/zacharysmith/2022/02/10/americans-lost-1-billion-to-romance-scammers-last-year-fbi-says/?sh=1702782961d1, 2022.

Investor.gov, s.v. “pump and dump schemes,” accessed December 18, 2022 https://www.investor.gov/introduction-investing/investing-basics/glossary/pump-and-dump-schemes. 2022.

McGraw, Phil, “Dr, Phil Show,” accessed December 18, 2022, https://www.drphil.com/shows/my-mom-is-delusional-she-thinks-shes-married-to-tyler-perry-and-has-sent-her-catfish-100000/, 2022.

Seon.io. dictionary, s.v. "auction fraud, accessed December 18, 2020, https://seon.io/resources/dictionary/auction-fraud/, 2022.

TechTarget.com, s.v. "crowdsourcing," accessed December 18, 2022, https//www.techtarget.com

Wikipedia, s.v., "crowdfunding, "accessed December 18, 2022, https://en.wikipedia.org/w/index.php?fulltext=1&profile=default&search=crowdfunding&title=Special:Search&ns0=1. 2022.

Wikipedia, s.v. "dark pattern," accessed December 18, 2022, https://en.wikipedia.org/wiki/Dark_pattern. 2022.

Wikipedia. s.v." exit scam," accessed December 18, 2022," https://en.wikipedia.org/wiki/Exit_scam. 2022.

Wikipedia. s.v. "romance scams," accessed December 18, 2022, https://en.wikipedia.org/wiki/Online_romance_scams. 2022

Wikipedia.org, "Know Your Enemy," https://en.wikipedia.org/wiki/Know_Your_Enemy:_Japan.

Yahoo.com, "17 Ways Making Yourself Target," accessed December 18, 2022. https://www.yahoo.com/now/17-ways-making-yourself-target-151419479/photo-youve-received-email-claiming-youre-220019617.html. 2022.

About the Author

Shelby Wagner is an award-winning author, church musician, public speaker, entertainer, and retired schoolteacher. She holds an MA from MSU and BA and BMus degrees from OU in Rochester, MI.

Born in Arkansas, Wagner grew up in Michigan, where she married and raised two children, and now lives in Southwest MI. She was recognized in the 1990-1991 Edition of Marquis' Who's Who in the Midwest for "outstanding achievement" and is currently a member of the International Society of Female Professionals, the Association of Authors, Writers, and Artists; the Professional Writers' Alliance, and the Independent Authors Network.
Please visit her website:
https://www.shelby-wagner.com and her channel:
YouTube.com/shelbywagner.

Another Book by author, Shelby Wagner:
Learning to Dance in the Rain – Surviving Grief, Internet Dating and Romance Scams
Now in its third printing. It is Wagner's personal story of loss and discovery as she learned to navigate grief, following the death of her husband of fifty years, began to reassess her options for the future and moved forward into a fulfilling and happy new life. Wagner's story is mind-blowing, and her suggestions are insightful and provocative.

Readers will learn the following and more:

- Why grieving is important and Tips for surviving the death of a loved one.
- Help assessing your future options.
- Making quality decisions
- Help in creating a plan of action
- Tips for successful online dating.
- Tips for thwarting romance scammers.

An Award-winning Memoir/Self-Help Book, Learning to Dance in the Rain II – Surviving Grief, Internet Dating and Romance Scams:

- **Living Now Book Awards Silver Medal.** Category: Relationships/Marriage, and Life-Changing Message
- **Book of the Year** by Independent Authors Network Finalist. Category: Grief/Hardship
- **Firebird Book Award Winner** – Category: Grief/Hardship
- **Royal Dragonfly** Winner
- **A Five Star Reader Review**
- **Four Star Literary Titan**
- **Feathered Quill Book Award** Finalist

- **Southern California Book Festival** – Honorable Mention
- **New England Book** Festival – Honorable Mention

Wagner has two new books on the way:

Suggestions for Dealing with Grief

Surviving Dating After 50

"Thank you for reading my book. It would make me very happy if you would post a book review on Amazon.com, BarnesandNoble.com or wherever applicable. I appreciate your help very much. Reviews are an author's lifeline and the major deciding factor for many book buyers. Thank you very much." – Shelby Wagner.

www.ingramcontent.com/pod-product-compliance
Lightning Source LLC
LaVergne TN
LVHW051923051126
851857LV00021B/2116